Alexandra Fenec

ORIGAMI BOOK
Animals

20 Easy Paper Folding Projects
with step by step instructions

Origami is a hobby with multiple benefits. Aside from being a fun and creative hobby with a beautiful finished product to look at, origami can be a soothing activity, fun to do in groups or a great teaching tool. The benefits of origami are only limited by your imagination!

Most people find the process of doing origami to be very relaxing and a great tool for reducing stress.

Creating origami sculptures increases focus of the mind while quieting the noise from a busy day. As skill with origami increases, the less thought is involved, creating a wonderful focus in which the worries of the day vanish. Concentrating on a simple task like folding paper and creating shapes becomes almost meditative, and can be a great way to release stress, reduce worry and anxiety, increase relaxation and promote a feeling of well-being.

Beginners should be sure to start off by creating very basic designs. Origami is an art that must be mastered in increments or it will seem overwhelming. Choose very simple designs, like the origami box, origami parrot, origami plane, and the origami ninja star, which are all 11 folds or under.

These designs will help beginners get a feel for the right ways to fold the paper and help them master the basics. It is important for beginners to practice these simple designs a few times, until they feel very comfortable with moving on to more difficult designs.

Once an artist is ready, it is then time to choose a few more difficult designs. Keep in mind that it is alright to struggle with some designs at first. Continuing to practice and work through any difficulties is the only way to master the art of origami. With some practice, most origami artists will find themselves improving and mastering the craft very quickly.

Share the hobby with friends and family. Origami is a fun and creative hobby that most people will enjoy. Sharing the skill with family and friends is a great way to create a mutual hobby. Additionally, many origami artists will find that teaching others the art of origami will work to strengthen their own skills.

This Origami Book contains:
• full-colored chemes with easy-to-follow instructions.
• 20 origami projects such as: fox, penguin, owl, shrimp, crab, lion and others.

This ebook is sure to keep kids engaged and happy for hours. They'll be so proud of their very first origami—and you'll be happy to display them!

The detailed instructions of Illustrattiva show you clear, step by step, how to create small active games with the origami art.

Easy to make and functional, you'll have fun in building small paper toys and playing with them.

Don't worry if they are not right the first time! We have to train!

If you are looking for simple, straight forward origami instructions, you have come to the right place. Here you will find out how to make every day objects with clear illustrations and simple instructions.

There are 20 fun-to-fold projects including a Pinguin, a Camel, a Dolphin, a Crow, a Giraffe and many others!

Have Fun!

Owl

1.

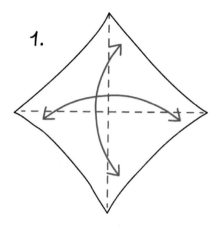

Fold in half twice to make creases and fold back

2.

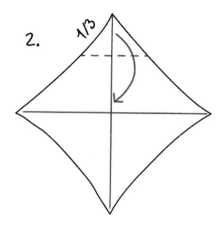

Fold in the dotted line

3.

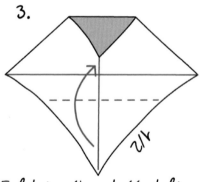

Fold in the dotted line

4.

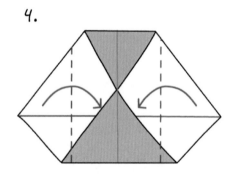

Fold in the dotted lines

5.

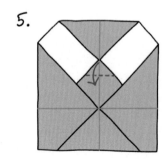

Fold in the dotted line to make the beak

6.

Draw eyes, feathers and finished

Fox

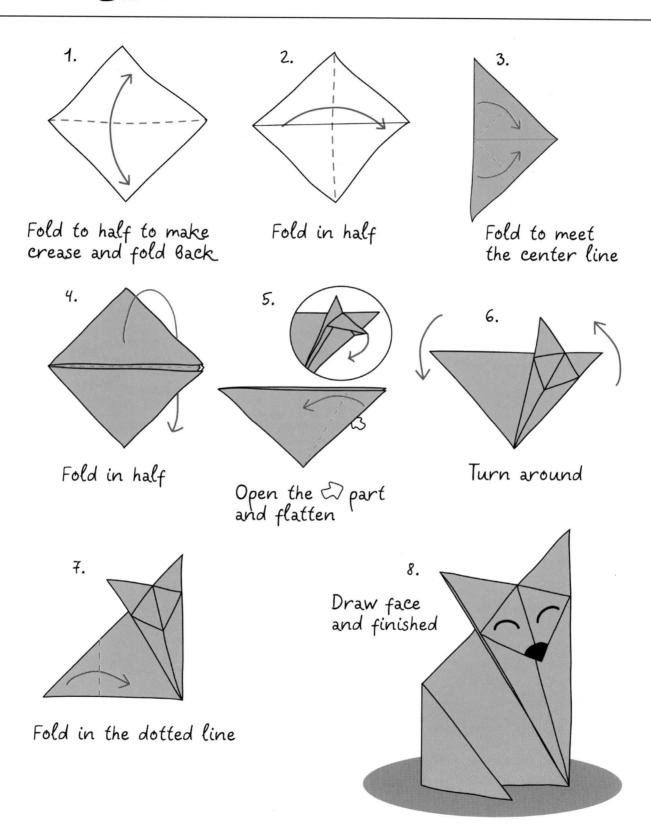

1. Fold to half to make crease and fold Back

2. Fold in half

3. Fold to meet the center line

4. Fold in half

5. Open the 🔖 part and flatten

6. Turn around

7. Fold in the dotted line

8. Draw face and finished

Snake

1.

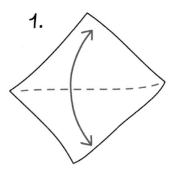

Fold to half to make crease and fold back

2.

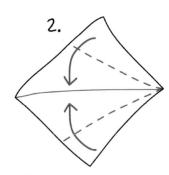

Fold in the dotted lines to meet the center line

3.

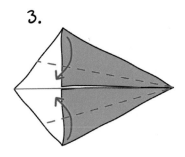

Fold in the dotted lines

4.

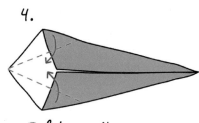

Fold in the dotted lines

5.

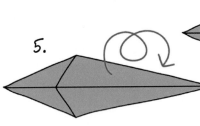

Turn over

6.

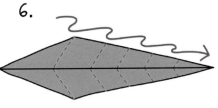

Step fold in the dotted lines

7.

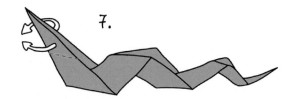

Hood fold in the dotted line

8.

Pocket fold in the dotted line

9.

Draw eyes and finished

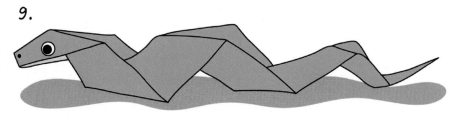

Bat

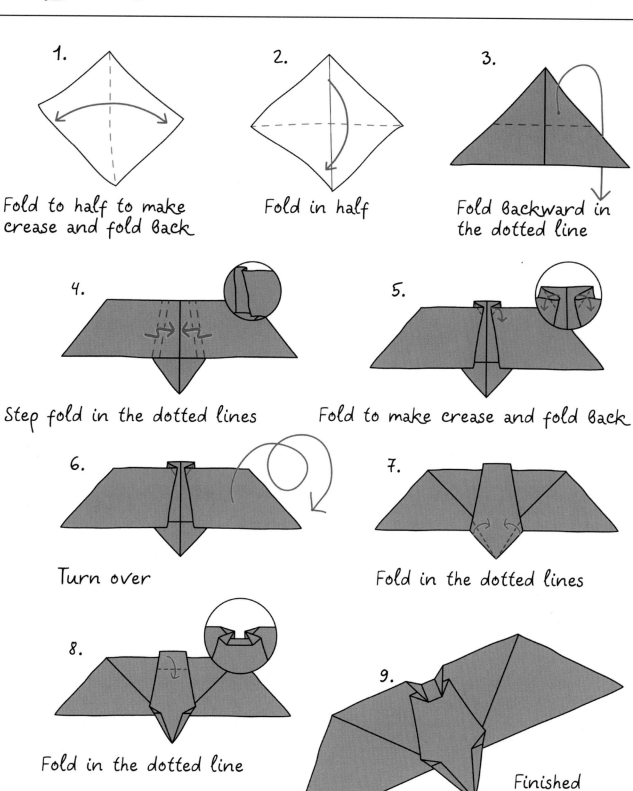

1. Fold to half to make crease and fold back

2. Fold in half

3. Fold backward in the dotted line

4. Step fold in the dotted lines

5. Fold to make crease and fold back

6. Turn over

7. Fold in the dotted lines

8. Fold in the dotted line

9. Finished

whale

1.

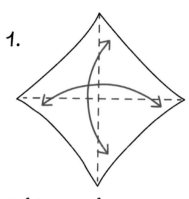

Fold in half twice to make creases and fold back

2. 1/3

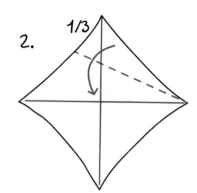

Fold in the dotted line

3.

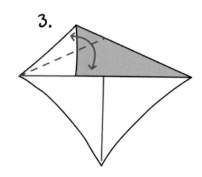

Fold in the dotted line and fold back

4.

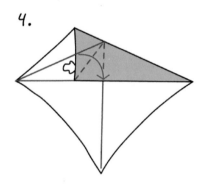

Open the 👉 part and flatten

5.

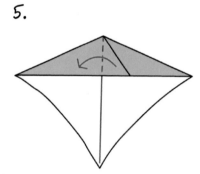

← Fold in the dotted line →

6.

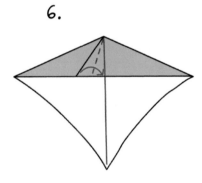

7.

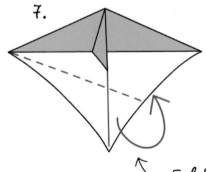

8.

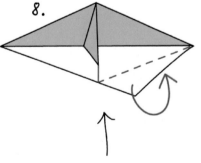

← Fold backward in the dotted line

9.

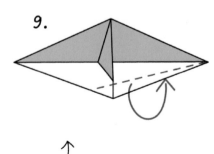

... almost done 👉

whale

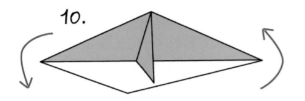

10.

Turn around

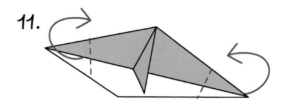

11.

Fold Backward

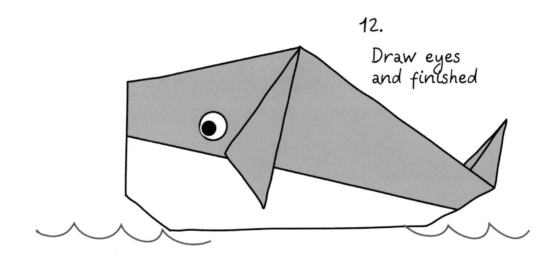

12.

Draw eyes
and finished

Lion

1.

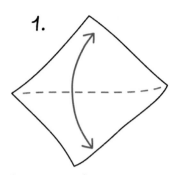

Fold to half to make
crease and fold Back

2.

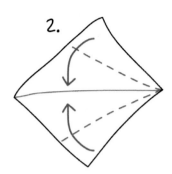

Fold in the dotted
lines to meet the center
line

3.

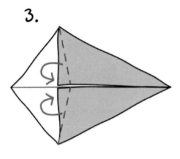

Fold Backward
in the dotted lines

4.

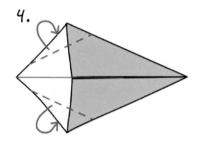

Fold Backward
in the dotted lines

5.

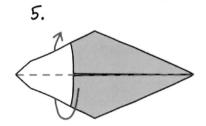

Fold in half

6.

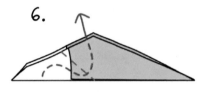

Pocket fold in the
dotted line

7.

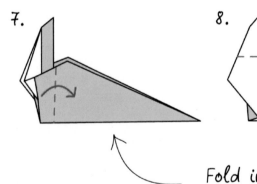

8.

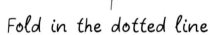

9.

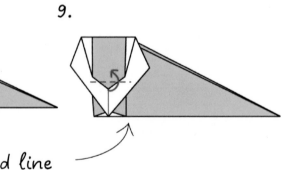

Fold in the dotted line

10. Fold in the dotted line

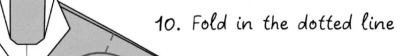

Lion

11.

12.

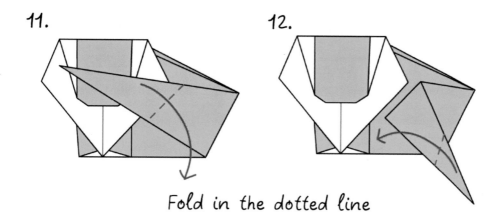

Fold in the dotted line

13. Draw face and finished

Crab

1.

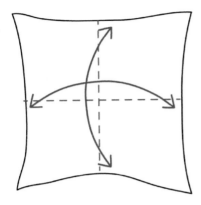

Fold in half twice to make creases and fold back

2.

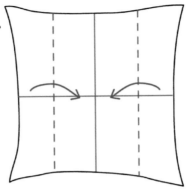

Fold to meet the center line

3.

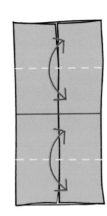

Fold to make crease and fold back

4.

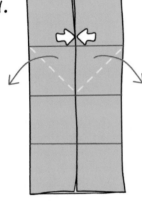

Open the 🖐 part and flatten

5.

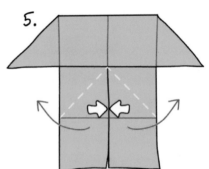

Open the 🖐 part and flatten

6.

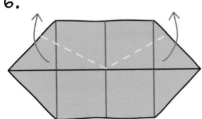

Fold in the dotted lines

7.

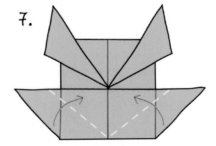

Fold in the dotted lines

8.

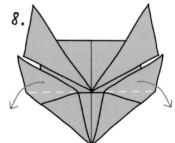

Fold in the dotted lines

Crab

9.

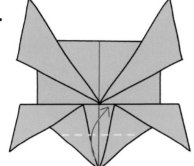

Fold in the dotted line

10.

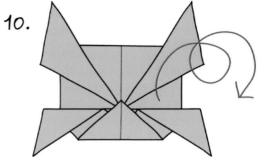

Turn over

11.

Draw eyes
and finished

Crow

1.

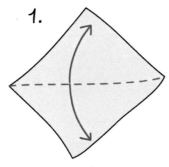

Fold to half to make crease and fold back

2.

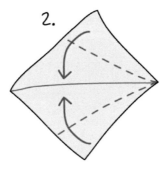

Fold in the dotted lines to meet the center line

3.

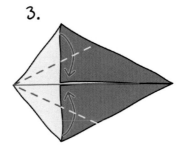

Fold in the dotted lines to meet the center line

4.

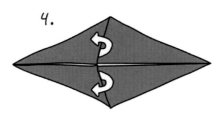

Open the pocket from 🖑

5.

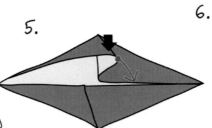

Flatten both pockets

6.

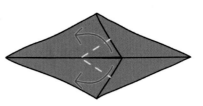

Fold in the dotted lines

7.

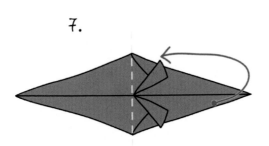

Fold backward in the dotted line

8.

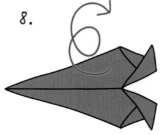

Turn over

9.

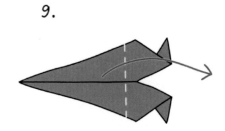

Fold in the dotted line

... almost done 🖘

Crow

10.

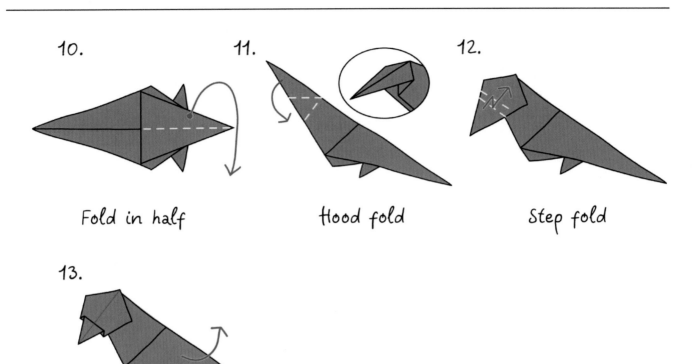

Fold in half

11.

Hood fold

12.

Step fold

13.

Adjust wings

14. Draw eyes and finished

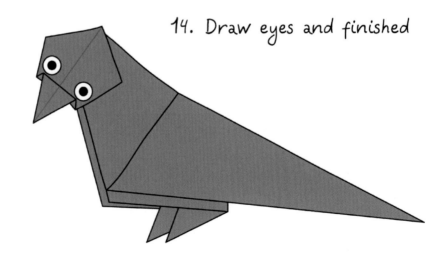

Dolphin

1.

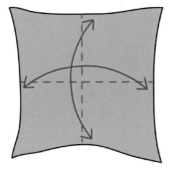

Valley-fold and unfold in half both ways. Turn over

2.

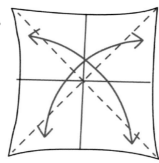

Valley-fold and unfold diagonally in half both ways

3.

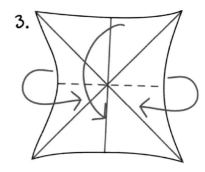

Collapse along existing creases

4.

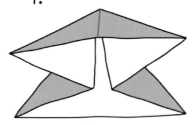

In progress

5.

2/3

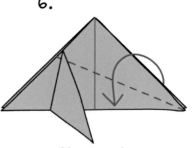

Valley-fold the front flap. Exact placement is not important

6.

Valley-fold

7.

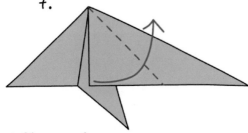

Valley-fold to make the dorsal fin. There is no guideline here, fold to taste

8.

Valley-fold

Dolphin

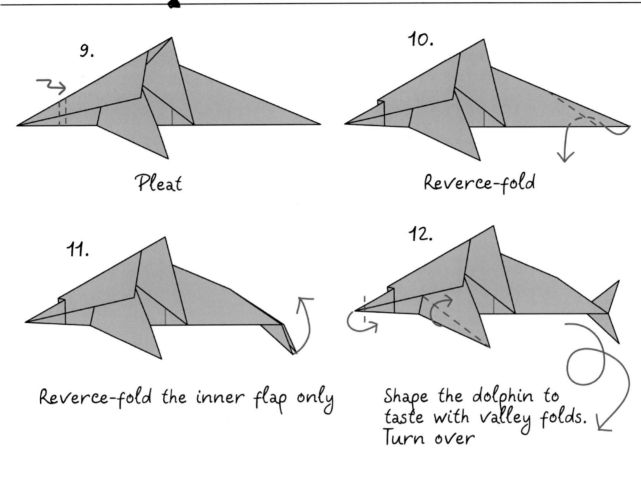

9.

Pleat

10.

Reverce-fold

11.

Reverce-fold the inner flap only

12.

Shape the dolphin to
taste with valley folds.
Turn over

13.

The dolphin ready to swim
away

Dachshund

1.

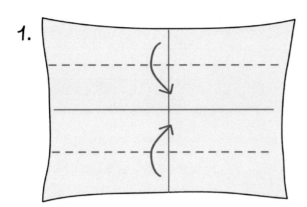

Fold to meet the center line

2.

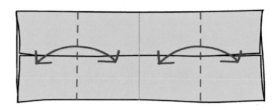

Fold to meet the center line
along the crease and fold back

3.

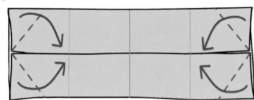

Fold to meet the center line

4.

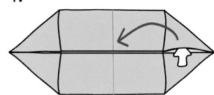

Open the 🐾 part
and flatten

5.

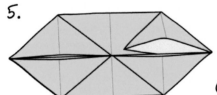

Follow the same step
as 4 to the other three

6.

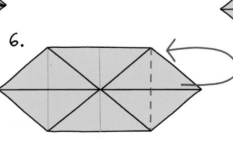

Fold backward in the
dotted line

7.

Fold in the
dotted lines

... almost done 🐾

Dachshund

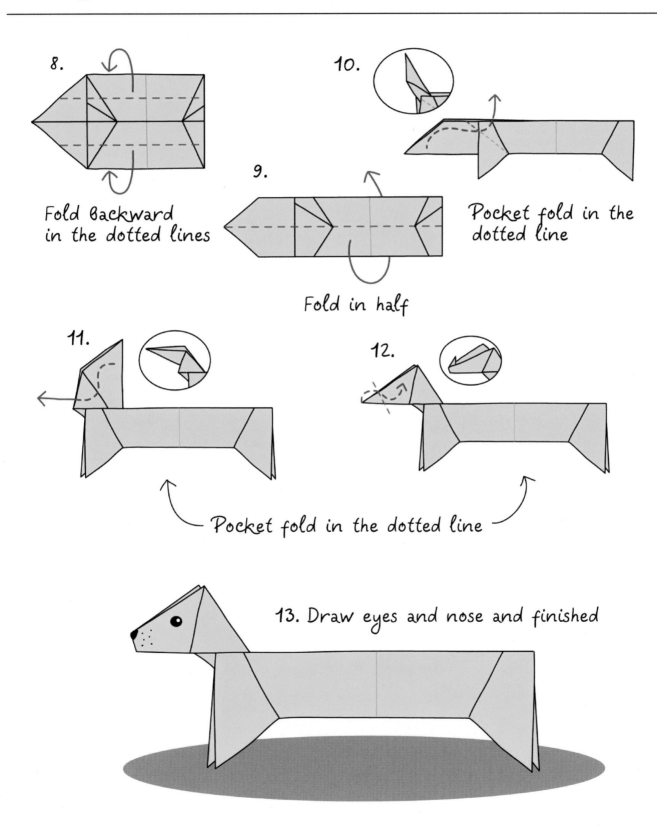

8.

Fold Backward
in the dotted lines

9.

Fold in half

10.

Pocket fold in the
dotted line

11.

12.

Pocket fold in the dotted line

13. Draw eyes and nose and finished

Seal

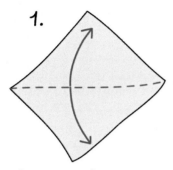

1.

Fold to half to make
crease and fold back

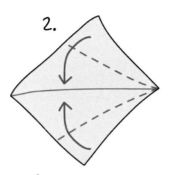

2.

Fold in the dotted
lines to meet the
center line

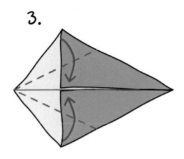

3.

Fold in the dotted
lines to meet the
center line

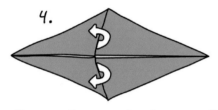

4.

Open the pocket from ⌐

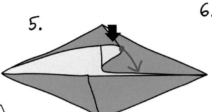

5.

Flatten both pockets

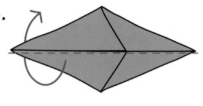

6.

Fold in half

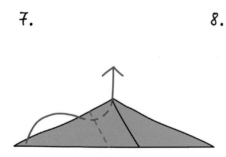

7.

Pocket fold in the
dotted line

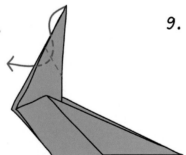

8.

Pocket fold in the
dotted line

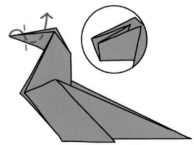

9.

Pocket fold in the
dotted line

... almost done ⌐

Seal

10.

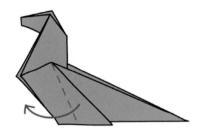

Fold forward in
the dotted line

11.

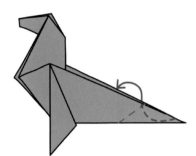

Pocked fold in
the dotted line

12.

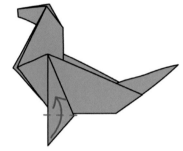

Fold forward in
the dotted line

13.

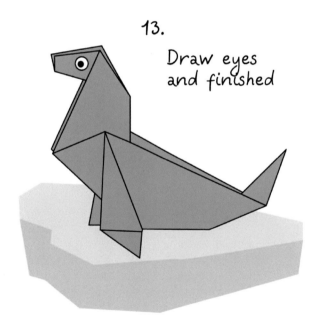

Draw eyes
and finished

Hippopotamus

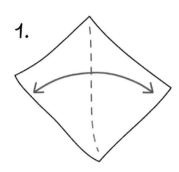

1.

Fold to half to make
crease and fold back

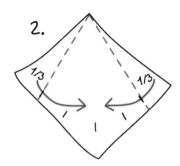

2.

Fold forward
in the dotted lines

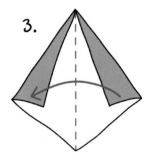

3.

Fold in half

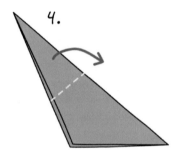

4.

Fold in the dotted line

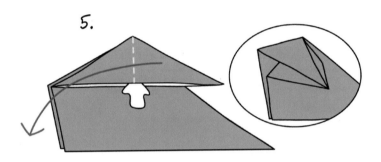

5.

Open the pocket
from 👈 and flatten

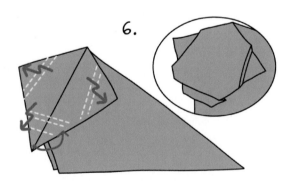

6.

Step fold in the dotted lines

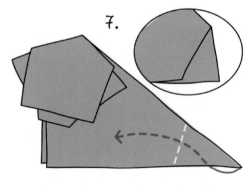

7.

Pocket fold in the
dotted line

... almost done 👉

Hippopotamus

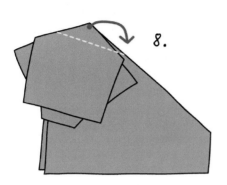

8.

Fold Backward

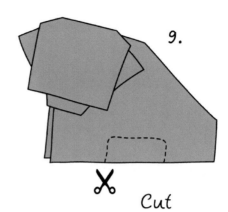

9.

Cut

10.

Draw eyes
and finished

Elephant

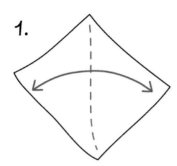

1.

Fold to half to make
crease and fold back

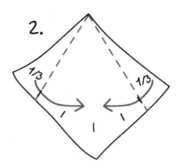

2.

Fold forward
in the dotted lines

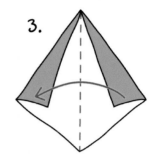

3.

Fold in half

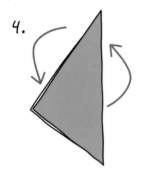

4.

Turn around

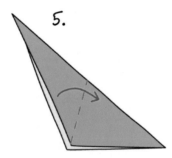

5.

Fold in the dotted line

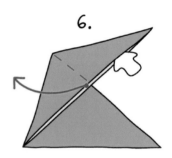

6.

Open from 👉

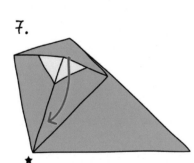

7.

Flatten at ★

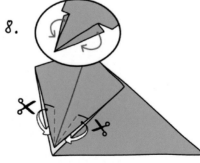

8.

Cut with a pair
of scissors and
fold inside

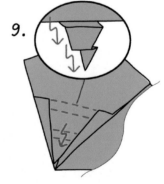

9.

Step fold

Elephant

10.

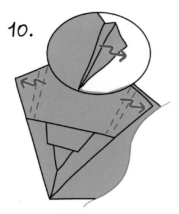

Step fold

11.

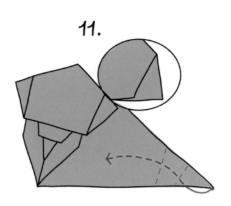

Pocket fold

12.

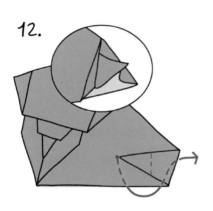

Pocket fold and pull out
the edge

13.

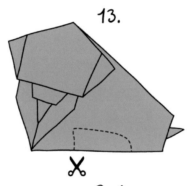

Cut

14.

Draw eyes and finished

Giraffe

1.
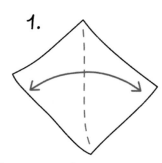

Fold to half to make crease and fold Back

2.
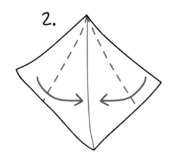

Fold in the dotted lines to meet the center line

3.
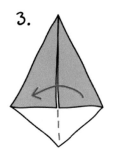

Fold in half

4.
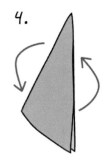

Turn around

5.
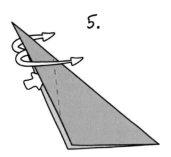

Open the pocket from ☞

6.
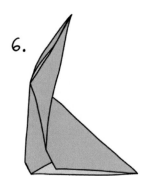

Hood fold

7.
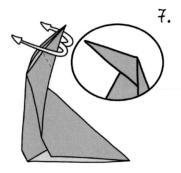

Hood fold inside

8.
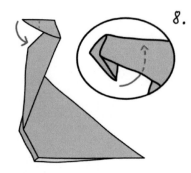

Pocket fold

9.
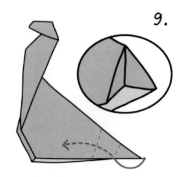

Pocket fold

... almost done ☞

Giraffe

10.

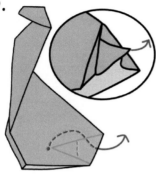

Pocket fold and
pull out the edge

11.

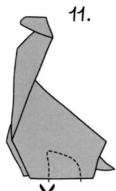

Cut with a pair
of scissors

12.

Draw eyes, spots
and finished

Penguin

1.
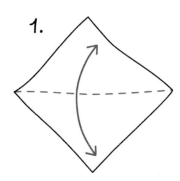

Fold to half to make crease and fold back

2.
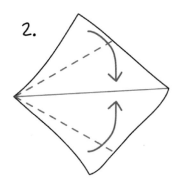

Fold forward in the dotted lines

3.
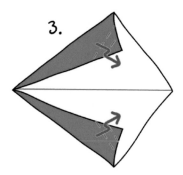

Step fold in the dotted lines

4.
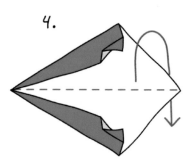

Fold backward in half

5.
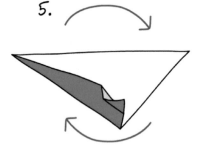

Turn around

6.
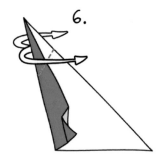

Hood fold in the dotted line

7.
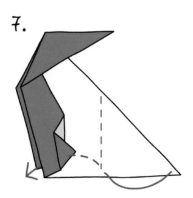

Pocket fold in the dotted line

8.

Pocket fold again

9.
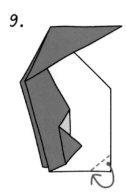

Fold inside in the other side, too

... almost done 👉

Penguin

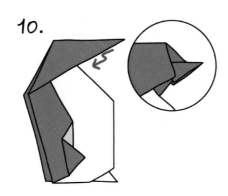

10.

Pocket fold and
step fold

11.

Draw eyes and finished

Flying Squirrel

1.

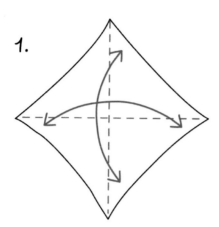

Fold in half twice to
make creases and
fold back

2.

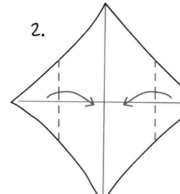

Fold to meet
the center line

3.

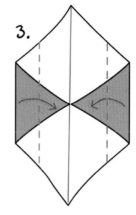

Fold to make crease
and fold Back

4.

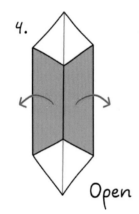

Open

5.

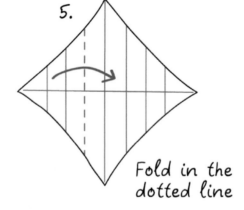

Fold in the
dotted line

6.

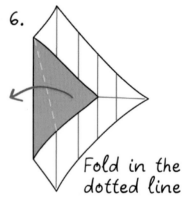

Fold in the
dotted line

7.

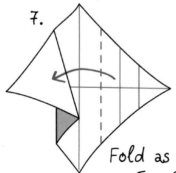

Fold as much
as 5 - 6

8.

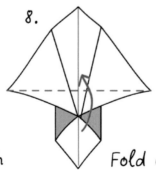

Fold in the
dotted line

9.

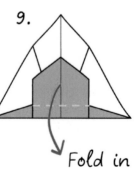

Fold in the
dotted line

Flying Squirrel

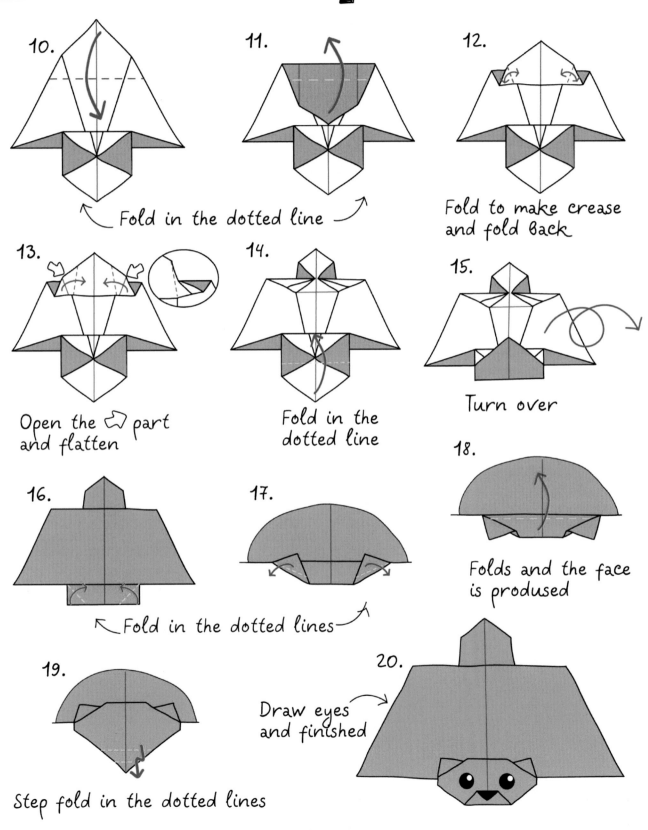

10.

Fold in the dotted line

11.

Fold in the dotted line

12.

Fold to make crease
and fold back

13.

Open the ☞ part
and flatten

14.

Fold in the
dotted line

15.

Turn over

16.

Fold in the dotted lines

17.

18.

Folds and the face
is prodused

19.

Step fold in the dotted lines

20.

Draw eyes
and finished

Camel

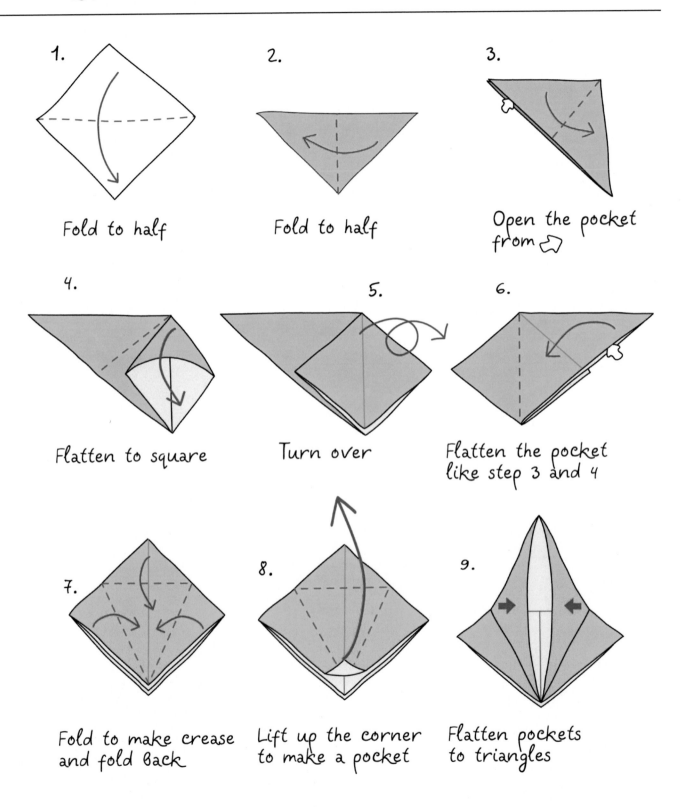

1. Fold to half

2. Fold to half

3. Open the pocket from 👆

4. Flatten to square

5. Turn over

6. Flatten the pocket like step 3 and 4

7. Fold to make crease and fold back

8. Lift up the corner to make a pocket

9. Flatten pockets to triangles

Camel

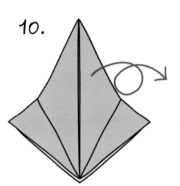

10.

Turn over

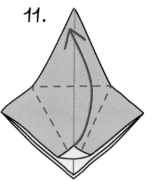

11.

Open and flatten the pocket like step 7, 8 and 9

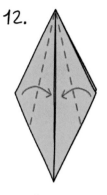

12.

Fold and the other side, too

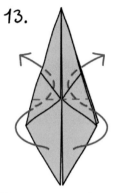

13.

Pocket fold in the dotted line

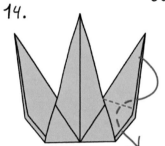

14.

Pocket fold in the dotted line

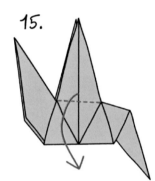

15.

Fold and the other side, too

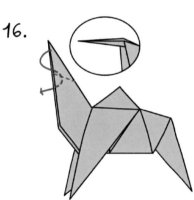

16.

Pocket fold

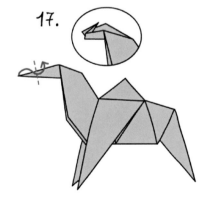

17.

Pocket fold

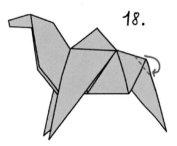

18.

Fold Backward and the other side, too

19. Draw eyes and finished

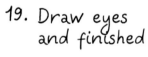

Turtle

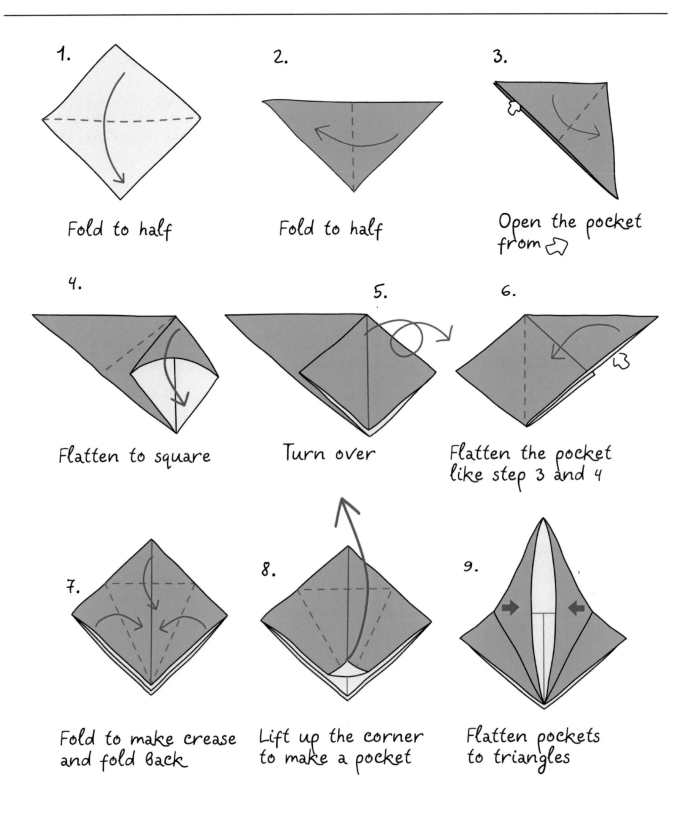

1. Fold to half

2. Fold to half

3. Open the pocket from 👆

4. Flatten to square

5. Turn over

6. Flatten the pocket like step 3 and 4

7. Fold to make crease and fold back

8. Lift up the corner to make a pocket

9. Flatten pockets to triangles

Turtle

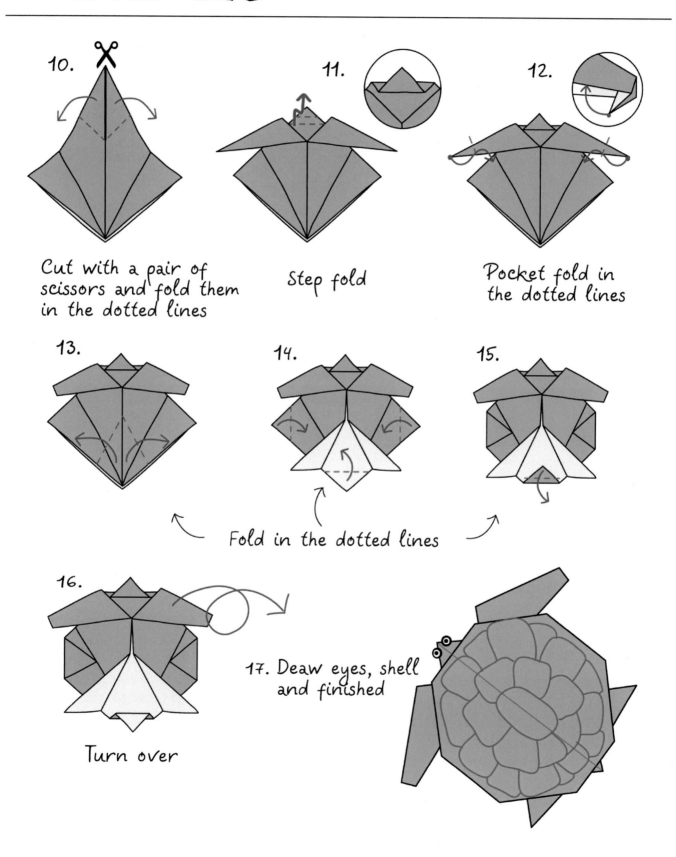

10. Cut with a pair of scissors and fold them in the dotted lines

11. Step fold

12. Pocket fold in the dotted lines

13.

14. Fold in the dotted lines

15.

16. Turn over

17. Deaw eyes, shell and finished

Crawfish

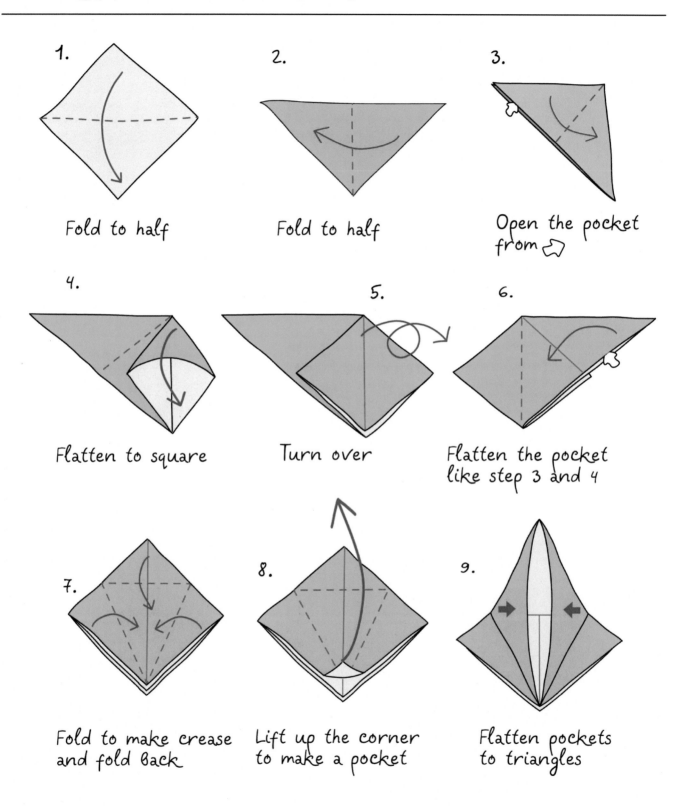

1. Fold to half

2. Fold to half

3. Open the pocket from 👉

4. Flatten to square

5. Turn over

6. Flatten the pocket like step 3 and 4

7. Fold to make crease and fold back

8. Lift up the corner to make a pocket

9. Flatten pockets to triangles

Crawfish

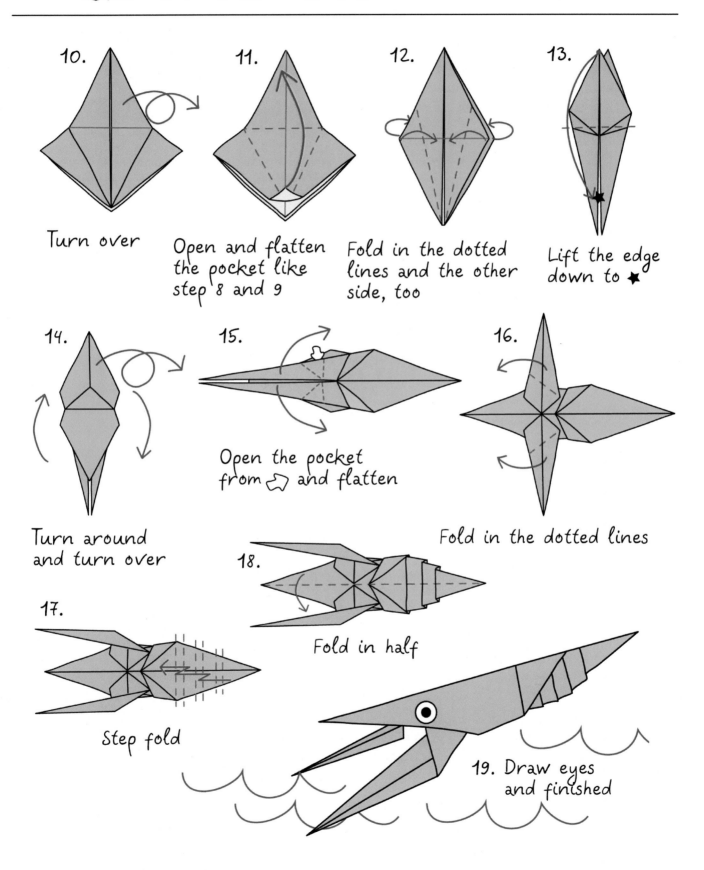

10.

Turn over

11.

Open and flatten the pocket like step 8 and 9

12.

Fold in the dotted lines and the other side, too

13.

Lift the edge down to ★

14.

Turn around and turn over

15.

Open the pocket from ⟲ and flatten

16.

Fold in the dotted lines

17.

Step fold

18.

Fold in half

19. Draw eyes and finished

Mantis

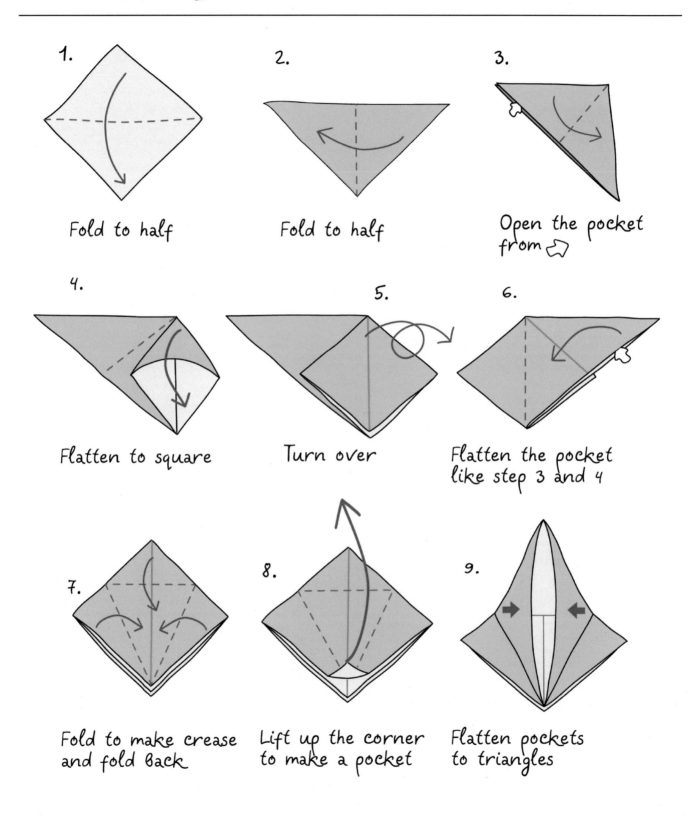

1. Fold to half

2. Fold to half

3. Open the pocket from ☞

4. Flatten to square

5. Turn over

6. Flatten the pocket like step 3 and 4

7. Fold to make crease and fold back

8. Lift up the corner to make a pocket

9. Flatten pockets to triangles

Mantis

10.

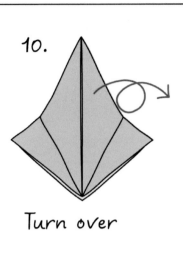

Turn over

11.

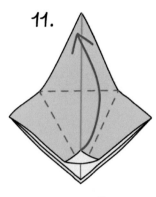

Open and flatten
the pocket like
step 7, 8 and 9

12.

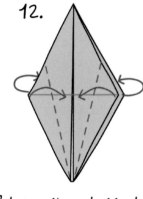

Fold in the dotted
lines and the other
side, too

13.

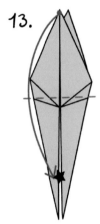

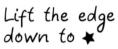

Lift the edge
down to ★

14.

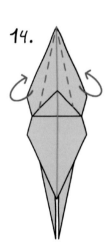

Fold Backward

15.

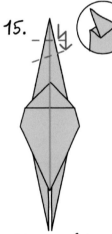

Step fold

16.

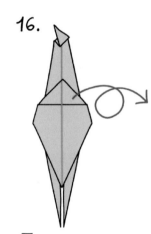

Turn over

17.

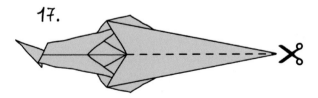

Cut with a pair of scissors

18.

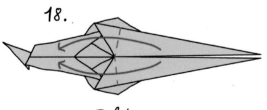

Fold

... almost done ⟳

Mantis

19.

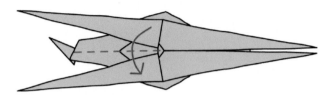

Fold in half

20.

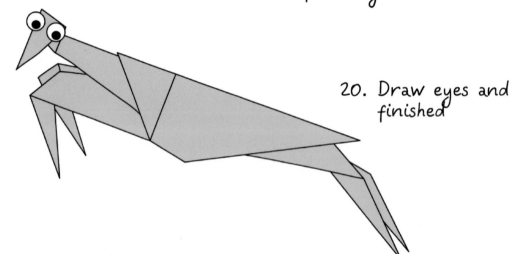

Fold in the dotted line
all four legs

20. Draw eyes and
finished